Write and Learn Sight Word Practice for Kids

SPEEDY
PUBLISHING

Speedy Publishing LLC
40 E. Main St. #1156
Newark, DE 19711
www.speedypublishing.com

Sight Words

a 5

big.............................7

can............................9

first 11

help 13

jump........................15

little.........................17

one...........................19

red...........................21

run 23

see 25

three 27

two..........................29

up 31

The boy is wearing **a** hat.

Trace the word.

a

Try it your own.

Use it in a sentence.

big

Trace the word.

big   big   big

Try it your own.

Use it in a sentence.

The pencil is **big**.

She **can** swim under the sea.

can

Trace the word.

 can   can   can

Try it your own.

Use it in a sentence.

Trace the word.

  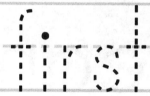

Try it your own.

_____

- - - - - - - - - - - - - - - - - - -

_____

Use it in a sentence.

_____

- - - - - - - - - - - - - - - - - - -

_____

Cute baby's **first** steps.

Firemen **help** putting out fire.

Trace the word.

Try it your own.

Use it in a sentence.

jump

Trace the word.

Try it your own.

Use it in a sentence.

The children are **jump**ing.

Little girl writing books.

Trace the word.

Try it your own.

Use it in a sentence.

one

Trace the word.

one   one   one

Try it your own.

Use it in a sentence.

Her **one** foot is injured.

The gift has a **red** ribbon.

Trace the word.

Try it your own.

Use it in a sentence.

run

Trace the word.

run   run   run

Try it your own.

Use it in a sentence.

The kids are **run**ning.

The diver have **see**n different
kinds of fishes.

see

Trace the word.

see

Try it your own.

Use it in a sentence.

three

Trace the word.

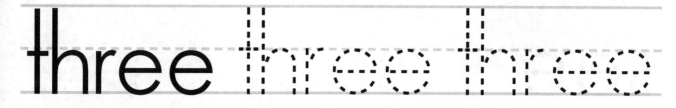

three three three

Try it your own.

Use it in a sentence.

Three kids are reading a book.

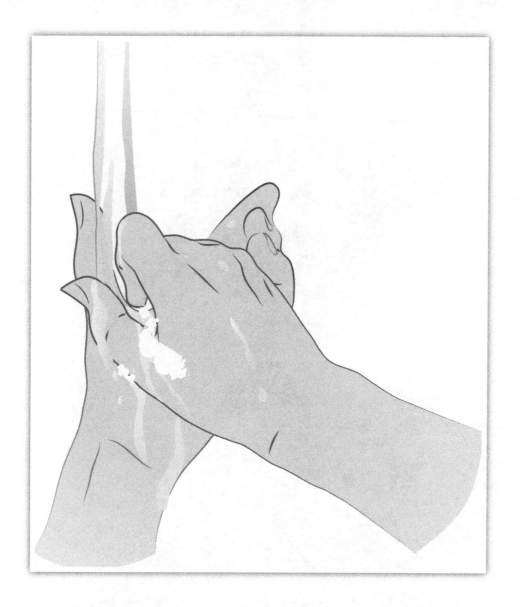

Wash your **two** hands.

two

Trace the word.

two   two   two

Try it your own.

Use it in a sentence.

up

Trace the word.

up   up   up

Try it your own.

Use it in a sentence.

The baby is looking **up**.

CPSIA information can be obtained
at www.ICGtesting.com
Printed in the USA
BVHW010232240821
615118BV00018B/271

9 781681 855820